Ferdinand Cheval

The Postman Who Delivered a Palace

written by **Anne Renaud**
illustrated by **Ana Salopek**

In a sleepy town in Southern France
stands a mysterious structure.

Is it a fortress?
A giant labyrinth?
The castle of a long-forgotten king?

It is, in fact, the work of one person.

A mailman named Ferdinand Cheval.

Who built it alone.

With nothing but his bare hands.

His will.

And a few tools.

For 33 years.

Today, this structure is a national treasure.

But it was not always so.

This is the story of its creation.

Ferdinand Cheval was a solitary man who spent his days delivering mail and daydreaming.

Every morning, Monsieur Cheval set out with a bag of mail, destined for the farmers and villagers scattered throughout the French countryside.

Until one day...
    when a rock...
        on his path...
            made him... stumble.

A "stumbling rock," you could say.

Monsieur Cheval marveled at this rock, for it was nothing like he had ever seen before.

"Nature can create such beauty," he thought as he dropped it into his mailbag. And there it sat until he returned home that evening, where he marveled at the rock some more.

In the days that followed, Monsieur Cheval walked his mail route and searched to find more stones as lovely as the one that had tripped him.

And when he did, he pushed them to the side of his path, then returned at the end of the day to collect them.

One evening, as he admired the stones he had collected, Monsieur Cheval had a thought.

In truth, he had many.

"If nature can create such beauty, could I too not create beauty with these stones? Could they not be a reminder that, despite my humble life, I was once here?"

And so, in his evenings, after collecting the stones he had pushed aside, Monsieur Cheval began to design... though he was not an architect, build... though he was not a builder, and sculpt... though he was not a sculptor.

The stones whispered to Monsieur Cheval and he listened.

First, the stones took on the shape of
a water fountain.
Then a grotto.
Then a passageway.

In the blazing heat of summer and the
biting cold of winter, his hands shaped
sandstone and limestone,
flint and river stones.

Learning as he went.
Inventing his own building techniques.
Failing until he succeeded.

Monsieur Cheval did not believe in
the word impossible.

Just as the sun rose each morning in the east,
so did a wall slowly rise.

Monsieur Cheval crafted more fountains, more grottos, and
more passageways, which he adorned with sculpted dogs and bulls,
squirrels and lions, and pointy-nosed foxes.

In the evenings, he perched on scaffolding and built and
shaped and carved by oil lamp.

He did not stop when his muscles ached.
Nor when his stomach grumbled.
Nor when his hands burned with lime.

Only when his eyelids grew heavy would he leave his stones
and go home.

Although he had traveled little, creatures and landscapes of far-off lands came to Monsieur Cheval in the images from the postcards, newspapers, magazines, and calendars he delivered.

Monsieur Cheval wove these images into his work.

Years went by and still Monsieur Cheval collected stones
on his mail route.

But he now attracted scornful stares.
His work was different.
It stood out.

It challenged the rules of architecture.
But this did not stop Monsieur Cheval.

While his neighbors grew cabbages and carrots,
he continued growing his dream to craft beauty
with his stones.

More years went by and still the stones whispered to Monsieur Cheval.

His wall was almost complete, with mummies and giants, sculpted palm trees, olive trees, fig trees, and cactus trees that tickled the sky.

Northern and southern walls now rose like an enormous labyrinth with more staircases, balconies, alcoves, and sculpted animals.

Monsieur Cheval began calling his work his palace. His Dream Palace. His Ideal Palace.

Now there rose a western wall with six columns, one for each letter in his name—Cheval.

His palace also had words, so many words, which Monsieur Cheval carved into the stone so his thoughts could be read.

Passerby, all that you see is the work of one peasant.

In creating this rock, I wanted to prove what the will can accomplish.

At every age, I learn that with persistence, hard work, and courage, one can assuredly achieve anything.

It is not time that passes; it is us.

By now, neighbors and passersby began seeing
his work differently.

Scornful looks softened.
Journalists wrote articles about him
in newspapers.

People had begun to see the beauty.

Only after thirty-three years had gone by did the stones
stop whispering to Monsieur Cheval.

He then took his "stumbling rock" and mounted it high
on his palace for everyone to see.

"I have crafted a thing of beauty just like nature. And despite
my humble life, there is now a reminder of my time here," he thought.

Monsieur Cheval never did believe in the word impossible.

Author's Note

The postman, Ferdinand Cheval, really did exist. He was born on April 19, 1836, in a French farming community called Charmes-sur-l'Herbasse. Orphaned by the time he was 19 and with little schooling, he first worked as a baker before taking a job as a postman in 1865.

In 1879, while delivering the mail, Ferdinand stumbled on a stone chiseled by nature and the passage of time. Fascinated by the beauty of the stone, he searched the area in the days that followed to see if he might find more stones like it. Traveling his mail route daily— a route more than 32 kilometers long— Ferdinand continued to collect stones he found particularly interesting and appealing. He was then inspired to build with them despite having no masonry or architectural skills.

What was the spark that inspired him to build? Perhaps it was to imitate nature and see if he too could create something of beauty. Maybe it was to prove he could leave his mark despite being poor and having little schooling. Or it may simply have been to display the stones to share their beauty with others. No one knows for sure. What we do know is that he built relentlessly for 33 years with only his hands and a few basic tools.

Completed in 1912, Ferdinand's palace still stands today in the small farming community of Hauterives. It measures 26 meters in length and ranges between 6.9 and 11 meters in height. Entirely shaped and carved by Ferdinand alone, it attracts over 180,000 people every year, who come to marvel at one man's dogged perseverance and creative spirit.

Ferdinand's palace received some recognition during his lifetime in architectural and newspaper articles. But only in later years did his work earn the acclaim it deserved. Painters, sculptors, and poets, such as Pablo Picasso, Andre Breton, and Max Ernst all drew inspiration from it, and represented it in their paintings, sketches, and poetry.

In 1969, it was named a Historical Monument by André Malraux, France's Minister for Cultural Affairs at that time, under Naïve Art. The structure, which is considered a national treasure, is now maintained by local masons, sculptors, and carvers who care for its preservation.

Ferdinand Cheval is today considered a worldwide forerunner of Naïve Architecture, an art form that defines itself as being architecture created by a person who lacks the formal education and training of a professional.

You can visit Monsieur Cheval's stone palace through a virtual tour at: www.facteurcheval.com

Anne Renaud

is an award-winning children's author who writes in both French and English. Her readers often ask her why she writes books. She tells them it is because she likes to do creative things and she finds writing to be a very creative exercise. It is also because she cannot dance well, sing well, juggle well, or do magic tricks, so she tries her best to write well. Anne stumbled upon the story of Ferdinand Cheval quite by chance while she was researching another one of her books. This often happens with writers. She found Ferdinand Cheval to be particularly inspiring because it told the story of how one man never gave up on his dream. Anne hopes this story will inspire children to pursue their dreams too.

Ana Salopek

lives in Ogulin, Croatia. She is a proud mom of a five-year-old girl who occasionally borrows her daughter's worldview on what truly matters in life. She creates and exhibits under her real name, Ana Salopek, as well as her pseudonym, gospođica ura. She uses books as her private time machine and creates using digital techniques as they give her more freedom. She believes that during the night, her legs lengthen as a giraffe's neck, allowing her to reach for the stars.